Love Letters from Jesus

Simple Truths and Practical Lessons
for Today's Christian...

from the Book of Revelation

Pastor Leonard P. Buelow

New Media Jet, LLC
United States of America

ISBN: 978-0615896397

To Carola, my faithful wife and helper
for almost 60 years . . .
you mean more to me than any words
could ever express.

All my love,
Leonard

SPECIAL THANKS

To Steven Buelow, my son.
Your consistent vision and enthusiasm is a
source of strength and encouragement.

To Katherine, my daughter-in-law.
Your caring spirit and eye for design
improves every project you touch.

To Marissa, my granddaughter.
Your willing heart and attention to detail
are appreciated more than you know.

CONTENTS

For many people, the Book of Revelation – the last book of the Bible – is very confusing. They find its strange symbols and images puzzling and mysterious. They misunderstand much of it and therefore apply unscriptural practices and beliefs. However, while there is much in the book that we cannot fully understand, it nevertheless contains important and practical lessons for today's Christian – and today's Christian churches. The book's very name means *a revealing*, a way to gain understanding. Its first verse tells us it was written to reveal *"things which must shortly take place."*

If you are confused by the Book of Revelation and would like to begin learning what it all means – and how its cast of mysterious characters all fit within Bible prophecy – then take to heart these sermons written and preached by Pastor Leonard Buelow. In them, you will find some of the most comforting words of the New Testament, as Jesus says, "Behold, I stand at the door and knock. If anyone hears My voice and opens the door, I will come in to him and dine with him, and he with Me." Revelation 3:20.

The Book of Revelation is one of five New Testament books written by the Apostle John. John's visions are like large, beautiful paintings. Like Jesus' parables, each picture has one point of focus that conveys a single lesson.

Many false teachers use Revelation as a source for some strange ideas about the last days. In this book of sermons, which rightly is called *Love Letters from Jesus,* Pastor Buelow, a faithful Lutheran Pastor of many years, presents clear Law/Gospel sermons that touch the heart and edify the soul.

The seven churches of Asia Minor were real congregations addressed at that time in history. However, Jesus' message to them is timeless, and these sermons relate Christ's message to the present day. The Law is proclaimed in all its truth and severity. The Gospel predominates, also proclaimed in all its truth and purity, bringing all sinners the assurance of God's love and forgiveness through the merits of Jesus Christ who lived, died and rose again for our salvation.

As a brother pastor in the Evangelical Lutheran Synod with 40 years of experience, I share a common background. Both Pastor Buelow and I were ordained in the same county (Shawano) of Wisconsin; only I was 16 years behind him. Having learned a valuable lesson in sermon writing *"to gather your flour wherever you can, but to make your own bread,"* I am always intrigued to read and be edified by the sermons of respected, confessional Lutheran Pastors.

Upon learning of this special sermon series from

the Book of Revelation, I requested and received these eight sermons from Pastor Buelow. Using the "flour" he so graciously shared, without the need of much "kneading," I delivered this series of sermons which he had written, and it edified both pastor and people.

Pastor Buelow is a gifted theologian who has both the ability to compose an edifying Law/Gospel sermon and the gift to preach it eloquently from the pulpit, reaching the head and touching the heart of all attentive listeners, young and old alike.

If you are a pastor looking to find an excellent example of homiletics, or to personally be edified through reading a scriptural sermon, or seeking to gather flour for your own sermon "baking," then by all means read this book.

If you are a layperson interested in better understanding the important and relevant lessons contained in the letters to the seven churches in the Book of Revelation, then, by all means, you have arrived at the proper place. Read, mark, learn and inwardly digest these exceptional sermons. You will truly be strengthened in your faith and advanced in your learning.

The evangelist John heard the voice of the Son of God. All who read these sermons will have the same experience, hearing God's voice in His Word. His Word is the only voice that should be heard in all churches today. Pastor Buelow has proclaimed this Word, thus serving as God's spokesman to proclaim both Law and Gospel to the people of our day.

Thankful for the opportunity to have experienced these sermons in advance of this publication, I presently await another planned publication of a sermon series by Pastor Buelow, titled *Mountaintop Experiences*. Everyone reading this book of sermons will be thankful that he has shared these pastoral blessings beyond his own personal parish. To God alone be all the glory!

Pastor Paul Schneider
Holy Scripture Lutheran Church
Midland, Michigan
Evangelical Lutheran Synod

"To Him who loved us and washed us from our sins in His own blood, and has made us kings and priests to His God and Father, to Him be glory and dominion forever and ever. Amen."

Revelation 1:5-6

"JOHN HEARD THE VOICE OF GOD!"
Revelation 1:8-18

Y ou may or may not be familiar with God's call to the young boy, Samuel. He was called to serve as a future prophet of God. As a young boy, Samuel was living and working in the temple area under the supervision of Eli the priest.

One evening, Samuel had gone to bed and suddenly he was awakened by a voice calling, "Samuel, Samuel!" He arose and ran into the room where Eli was sleeping and he said, "Here I am. You called me." Eli said, "I didn't call you. Go back to bed." He lay down and again the voice called, "Samuel, Samuel!" He arose again and ran into Eli's room and said, "Here I am. You called me." Eli said, "I did not call you. Go back to bed." Samuel returned to his room and lay down and soon he heard the voice for a third time, "Samuel, Samuel!" He arose and ran to Eli and said, "Here I am, for you did call me!"

At that point Eli suspected that it was the voice of God. He instructed Samuel to go back to bed and told him that if he heard the voice again, he should respond, "Speak, Lord, for Your servant hears," I Samuel 3:9.

Samuel went back to bed and indeed the Lord called again, "Samuel, Samuel!" and he responded, "Speak, for Your servant hears." I Samuel 3:10. Samuel was being prepared by God to fulfill a specific role in the leadership of the Lord's people.

Today, we turn our attention to a report recorded in the last Book in the New Testament of the Bible where we learn how,

"JOHN HEARD THE VOICE OF GOD!"

We read in the Book of Revelation, chapter one, verses eight through eighteen: "'I am the Alpha and the Omega, the Beginning and the End,' says the Lord, 'who is and who was and who is to come, the Almighty.' I, John, both your brother and companion in the tribulation and kingdom and patience of Jesus Christ, was on the island that is called Patmos for the Word of God and for the testimony of Jesus Christ. I was in the Spirit on the Lord's Day, and I heard behind me a loud voice, as of a trumpet, saying, 'I am the Alpha and the Omega, the First and the Last,' and, 'What you see, write in a book and send it to the seven churches which are in Asia: to Ephesus, to Smyrna, to Pergamos, to Thyatira, to Sardis, to Philadelphia, and to Laodicea.' Then I turned to see the voice that spoke with me. And having turned I saw seven golden lampstands, and in the midst of the seven lampstands One like the Son of Man, clothed with a garment down to the feet and girded about the chest with a golden band. His head and hair were white like wool, as white as snow, and His eyes like a flame of fire; His feet were like fine brass, as if refined in a furnace, and His voice as the sound of many waters; He had in His right hand seven stars, out of His mouth went a sharp two-edged sword, and His countenance was like the sun shining in its strength. And when I saw Him, I fell at His feet as dead. But He laid His right hand on me, saying to me, 'Do not be afraid; I am the First and the Last. I am He who lives, and was dead, and behold, I am alive forevermore. Amen. And I have the keys of Hades and of Death.'"

PART I: THE VOICE OF AUTHORITY

Our sermon today is an introduction to what we will consider during the coming seven weeks. Each week, we will direct our attention to a letter written to one of the seven churches in Asia Minor. These letters are recorded in the verses and chapters that follow our text. For the next seven weeks, you might want to read those letters at home before coming for worship.

Our text deals with a number of specifics. The author identifies himself for the third time specifically as, "John." He identifies himself as a "brother," that is, a Christian brother in the faith, who was in tribulation at the time, that is, suffering because he was teaching the Word of God and proclaiming the Christian faith.

He specifically tells us when he heard the voice of God, "I was in the Spirit on the Lord's Day, and heard behind me a great voice, as of a trumpet." The call of God came to him on the Lord's Day, on a Sunday, the day the early Christians had chosen as their day of worship, a custom which we continue.

He also specifically tells us where he was when he heard the voice of God. He was on the island of Patmos. It is a barren island off the coast of present day Turkey, about ten miles long and six miles wide at its widest point. It was used by the Roman government as a place of exile for prisoners. (It was much like the island of Alcatraz which our government used as a Federal prison for many years.)

According to reliable church historians, John was sent into exile on the island of Patmos by the Roman government during the reign of Domitian in about the year 95 A.D. and he was released about one year later after Domitian's death.

John was exiled to the island of Patmos because he preached a message of repentance and a message of salvation through the Gospel of Jesus Christ alone. This is the same John who wrote that Jesus identified

Himself as the only Savior when He said, "I am the Way, the Truth, and the Life. No one comes to the Father except through Me," John 14:6. That upset the Roman rulers to no end!

Study the history of Scripture and secular history, and you will see how often people in government, and others too, get upset by the Word of God, for example, with the Ten Commandments and with the Gospel of Jesus Christ. In our own land, the posting of the Ten Commandments in public places upsets many people in government and others too. But then it isn't surprising when you see how many of these people live. After all, the Ten Commandments do say, "Thou shalt . . . and thou shalt not!" and that upsets a lot of people because it convicts them of their sinful way of life!

The Gospel is equally upsetting to many because it tells us that we are saved and go to heaven, not by what we do, but by God's grace for Christ's sake through faith alone. To show how far some people with authority go, I am reminded of a report recently that a man, I believe it was in New Jersey, was denied the privilege of having the reference of a certain Bible verse on his automobile registration plate because it might offend somebody. I believe that he requested something like John 3:16, which, as all of you know, or maybe all of you don't know, reads, "For God so loved the world that He gave His only begotten Son, that whoever believes in Him should not perish but have everlasting life."

Think also of all of the anti-God, anti-Christian, and anti-religion movements in our own country. We boast of the fact that we have freedom of religion, but there is also an organization known as Freedom From Religion. You cannot talk about God in our public classrooms, however a teacher, even here in our own vicinity, can require the students in the classroom to read aloud from books that use the name of God in vain. A moment for silent prayer in the classroom is taboo and your sports teams should not pray either!

This reminds me of a man whom I visited in the hospital about a year and a half or two years ago, who asked me not to pray or to read any Scripture to him. He said that there is no God and that he didn't need one. He admitted that he was reared as a Lutheran and that he once had believed in God until he went to the university and there the professors convinced him that there is no God and no need for a God. The man died! And you can count on it; he had to face God!

The God whom he had to face, and whom he was not prepared to face, is the same God, the only one and true God, before whom each of us must appear, be it on the day of death or Judgment Day, whichever comes first. We will hear His voice when He comes, as we are told just prior to our text, "Behold, He is coming with clouds, and every eye will see Him, even they who pierced Him. And all the tribes of the earth will mourn because of Him," Revelation 1:7. There will be mourning by millions who are not prepared to stand before God because they reject Jesus Christ as the Son of God and the only Savior of sinners!

The voice of God that John heard was the voice of authority. Speaking of His authority, Jesus said on another occasion, "Most assuredly, I say to you, the hour is coming, and now is, when the dead will hear the voice of the Son of God; and those who hear will live. For as the Father has life in Himself, so He has granted the Son to have life in Himself, and has given Him authority to execute judgment also, because He is the Son of Man. Do not marvel at this; for the hour is coming in which all who are in the graves will hear His voice and come forth," John 5:25-29.

The voice that spoke with authority gave specific instructions to John to write. "What you see, write in a book and send it to the seven churches which are in Asia." The voice did not convey just a personal message. As the called servant of God, John was commissioned to write a specific message to each of the seven churches in Asia Minor.

PART II: THE VOICE OF GOD IDENTIFIED

Now we want to direct our attention to the specifics of the voice that identified itself both in words and appearance. In one place the voice is identified as "a loud voice, as of a trumpet," and in another place, "His voice (was) as the sound of many waters." It was an impressive voice, a voice that would get one's attention. And it did just that. John turned around to see who was speaking.

The voice identified Himself as Alpha and Omega, the Beginning and the End, who is and who was and who is to come, the Almighty. It was none other than the almighty God who was speaking. It was He who in the beginning created heaven and earth. It was He of whom we confess in the Creed, "I believe in God the Father almighty Maker of heaven and earth."

It was the voice of the almighty God who appeared to other children of God in times past. For example, He appeared to Abraham repeatedly and told him that he and Sarah would have a son in their old age, who would be an ancestor of the promised Savior, the Lord Jesus Christ. When Abraham questioned that possibility because of his and Sarah's age, the Lord said, "I am Almighty God; walk before Me and be blameless," Genesis 17:1. God said, "Trust Me! It's going to happen!"

This same God appeared to Moses in a burning bush and called, "'Moses, Moses!' And he said, 'Here I am.' . . . Moreover (God) said, 'I am the God of your father – the God of Abraham, the God of Isaac, and the God of Jacob," Exodus 3:4,6. That meant He was the God of promises, promises made and promises kept. He was the God who promised to one generation after another that He would send a Savior into the world. God kept that promise. "When the fullness of the time had come, God sent forth His Son, born of a woman, born under the law, to redeem those who were under the law, that we might receive the adoption as sons," Galatians 4:4-5.

As God the Father spoke to John, so also the Son of God and Son of Man spoke with him. The Son of God identified Himself with the same and similar titles. "I am the Alpha and Omega, the First and the Last," and, "I am He who lives, and was dead, and behold, I am alive forevermore." Alpha and Omega are the first and last letters of the Greek alphabet. Christ is the First and the Last; He is the first Savior and the last Savior, and the only Savior. He is our ever-living Savior and our ever-living Lord.

Indeed, He came into this world as a little baby. The government was not happy with Him. King Herod regarded Him as a threat to his throne and tried to kill Him. His own people on occasion tried to stone Him and push Him off a cliff. But they could not do anything to Him until God's hour had come. When the Savior had fulfilled all things as Scripture had predicted, then they could take Him captive, and He was condemned and crucified. He died! But in our text He identifies Himself with the words, "I am He who lives, and was dead, and behold, I am alive forevermore."

He died! And by His death He sacrificed Himself to take away all our sins. God's Word assures us, "The blood of Jesus Christ His Son cleanses us from all sin," I John 1:7. There is no sin so great or grievous, so horrible or heinous, so ugly or repulsive that it cannot be forgiven. "(God) made Him who knew no sin to be sin for us, that we might become the righteousness of God in Him," II Corinthians 5:21. "God demonstrates His own love toward us, in that while we were still sinners, Christ died for us . . . If when we were enemies we were reconciled to God through the death of His Son, much more, having been reconciled, we shall be saved by His life," Romans 5:8,10.

He died, but He rose again. He came forth victoriously from the grave. He conquered sin, death and hell. It is our living Lord who speaks in and to His churches.

In our text John speaks of Him as the Son of God and Son of Man who was majestically arrayed and adorned as a symbol of purity and power and who is present among His people with His Word and Sacraments. He is present now as we hear His Word.

The seven golden lampstands referred to in our text represented the seven churches in Asia Minor. The seven stars represented the seven messengers or pastors of the churches. Out of the Savior's mouth "went a sharp two-edged sword." The writer of the Letter to the Hebrews tells us that, "The Word of God is living and powerful, and sharper than any two-edged sword," Hebrews 4:12.

In his Letter to the Ephesians, the apostle Paul emphasizes the importance of the Word of God, when he writes, "Take up the whole armor of God, that you may be able to withstand in the evil day, and having done all, to stand. Stand therefore, having girded your waist with truth, having put on the breastplate of righteousness, and having shod your feet with the preparation of the Gospel of peace; above all, taking the shield of faith with which you will be able to quench all the fiery darts of the wicked one. And take the helmet of salvation, and the sword of the Spirit, which is the Word of God," Ephesians 6:13-17.

John heard the voice of God. We hear His voice in His Word. His Word is the only voice that should be heard in the churches. That will become very clear to us during the next seven weeks as we visit the churches of Asia Minor and read and study their Letters. God grant it! AMEN!

For further thought and discussion:

◆ Have you ever found the Book of Revelation to be confusing, or found yourself at a loss for words in a conversation about the Book?

◆ John was persecuted for practicing his faith and proclaiming the Gospel of Jesus Christ. Have you ever experienced pain or persecution because of your faith? (Page 20)

◆ Are you prepared to face the Lord at the end of your life? Why or why not? (Pages 22-23)

◆ What did Jesus say about himself? How did he identify Himself to John? (Page 25)

◆ How do you feel knowing that "the blood of Jesus Christ cleanses us from all sin?" (Page 26)

◆ In the Book of Revelation, what do the seven golden lampstands represent? The seven stars? The two-edged sword? (Page 27)

"A CHURCH THAT LOST ITS FIRST LOVE!"
Revelation 2:1-7

In our introductory sermon we learned how the apostle John heard the voice of God while he was living in exile on the island of Patmos, and that he received from the Lord specific instructions to write a letter to each of the seven churches in Asia Minor.

Today, we continue that series of sermons and direct our attention to the first of the seven Letters, the Letter to the church in Ephesus, where we hear about,

"A CHURCH THAT LOST ITS FIRST LOVE!"

Our text is recorded in the Book of Revelation, chapter two, verses one through seven: "To the angel of the church of Ephesus write, 'These things says He who holds the seven stars in His right hand, who walks in the midst of the seven golden lampstands: I know your works, your labor, your patience, and that you cannot bear those who are evil. And you have tested those who say they are apostles and are not, and have found them liars; and you have persevered and have patience, and have labored for My name's sake and have not become weary. Nevertheless I have this against you, that you have left your first love. Remember therefore from where you have fallen; repent and do the first works, or else I will come to you quickly and remove your lampstand from its place – unless you repent. But this you have, that you hate the deeds of the Nicolaitans, which I also hate. He who has an ear, let him hear what the Spirit says to the churches. To him who overcomes I will give to eat from the tree of life, which is in the midst of the Paradise of God.'"

PART I: A QUESTION PRECEDED BY COMMENDATION

Our text contains the first of seven public pastoral letters written to the seven churches in Asia Minor. Each of the seven Letters has a similar outline. Each Letter deals with the spiritual condition of a congregation located in a particular place. Each Letter contains a call to repentance and faithfulness. Each Letter closes with the promise of a blessing for those who take to heart what is written.

As we heard in the introductory sermon, the congregations were represented in John's vision by "seven golden lampstands," or candlesticks. That symbolized how precious those congregations were in the Lord's sight. Also in each instance we are told that the Lord Jesus walks in the midst of His congregations. Each of the Letters was to be taken to the people by the "seven stars," or "angels" as they were also called. Those expressions referred to the leaders or the pastors of the congregations.

In the case of the congregation at Ephesus, the apostle Paul was once such a "star" for the congregation. Paul had founded the congregation and he worked there very successfully for three years in spite of many difficulties and great opposition. Other people, such as Aquila and Priscilla, Apollos, and Timothy followed in Paul's footsteps and worked in the congregation at Ephesus also. All of them were concerned about carrying out the great commission of Christ, the preaching of the message of salvation to the people of Ephesus.

This is the same congregation to whom the apostle Paul wrote, "For by grace you have been saved through faith, and that not of yourselves; it is the gift of God, not of works, lest anyone should boast. For we are His workmanship, created in Christ Jesus for good works, which God prepared beforehand that we should walk in them," Ephesians 2:8-10.

The people who labored for the Lord in the church at Ephesus were very faithful and their labors were not in vain. In the Letter of John recorded in our text to the Ephesian Christians, the members of the congregation were commended. They worked hard. They were patient people. They practiced Christian discipline among the members. They carefully studied Christian doctrine. When false teachers, such as the Nicolaitans, came to them, they distinguished between truth and error and they rejected the false teachings. They suffered and endured the disgrace that was heaped upon them by the Ephesian people who worshiped heathen gods. Patiently, they endured the persecution that came to them as it did to so many people in the early Christian church.

Now, if you look at this more closely, faith in Christ, true Christian living, faithful service to the Lord, Christian discipline among the members, the determination to continue with Christian teaching and practice, patience and perseverance, are all characteristics of a Christian congregation.

These are the virtues that must be found among us also as members of a Christian congregation. These are things for which we also as members of a Christian congregation should be commended. We often remind ourselves of this when we speak of our congregation as being a Christian family. People who visit our congregation frequently comment on our Christian friendliness as a family. That is very commendable, encouraging, and inviting. And for us, as a people, it should be very genuine; it should not be something "put on." It should be real, not fake!

The compliments given to the congregation at Ephesus came from Him who identified Himself in the verses preceding our text with the words, "I am the First and the Last. I am He who lives, and was dead, and behold, I am alive forevermore." It was Jesus, who had been crucified and who died, but who now is the risen Redeemer and our ever-living Lord, who addressed the people in that place. The Son of God complimented and commended the people of the Ephesian congregation.

That has great importance and significance also for us. It is not just the nice things we think and say of ourselves or the nice things others say about us that are so important. We must know that what we are doing as a congregation is God-pleasing and to God's glory and that it is acceptable to our Lord and Savior Jesus Christ.

Today, we remember how four years ago about fifty Builders For Christ and their spouses appeared on the scene and began building this house of God. As we think back, many nice things can be said about us as a congregation. We can be commended for our Christian faith, for our Christian works, for our labors of love in our homes, in the congregation, and in our community. We can say that we compare favorably with what was written to the congregation at Ephesus.

Now listen once more to the words of the Lord's commendation to the Ephesian congregation: "I know your works, your labor, your patience, and that you cannot bear those who are evil. And you have tested those who say they are apostles and are not, and have found them liars; and you have persevered and have patience, and have labored for My name's sake and have not become weary."

Now, think of applying these words to ourselves. Next to our Christian faith, our trust in Christ as our Lord and Savior, we should have Christian virtues of which a most prominent one is – patience, Christian patience and more patience! We cannot bear all the evil in the world around us. However, we do not become weary; we don't give up! We put everything that we hear and see to the test and we continue with the truth, the truth of God's Word. The Savior and His Word should be and remain our first love. However is it always that way?

PART II: A QUESTION THAT SEARCHES THE SOUL

After commending the people in the Ephesian congregation, the Lord instructed John to write some shocking words: "Nevertheless I have this against you, that you have left your first love." In spite of the many praiseworthy things that could be said about the congregation, a sad statement had to be added. They had left their first love.

Does this mean that they had completely forsaken Christ as their Lord and Savior? No, because if that were the case, they would have ceased to be a Christian congregation. They still were very much concerned about Christian doctrine and teaching. They did not tolerate false teachers. But they had lost their first love. Their love, zeal and devotion for the Lord and for the work of the church had disappeared. They once had been devoted church workers, but their love for the Lord and His church had cooled off.

We also see this happen in churches today. People become members of a congregation. They are all excited. They are, as we say, "gung ho!" However it is only for a short time, and then you see and hear less and less of them. And then you see them no more! Of course, this is nothing new.

This happened even during the days of the Savior's public ministry. Jesus had many followers in different places on occasion, but they did not always continue to follow Him. On one occasion, when He spoke about Himself as the Bread of Life from heaven, Scripture tells us, "Many of His disciples, when they heard this, said, 'This is a hard saying; who can understand it?' . . . From that time many of His disciples went back and walked with Him no more.

(They lost their first love.) Then Jesus said to the twelve, 'Do you also want to go away?' But Simon Peter answered Him, 'Lord, to whom shall we go? You have the words of eternal life. Also we have come to believe and know that You are the Christ, the Son of the living God,'" John 6:60,66-69.

What a beautiful confession of faith. Yet, on the first Maundy Thursday evening after Christ was taken captive, when Peter was confronted three times for being a disciple of Jesus, he also lost his first love and denied His Lord and Savior. He swore up and down that he never knew who Jesus was! How quickly his love for his Lord turned cold!

After Jesus' resurrection and before He ascended into heaven, He dealt with Peter to restore that first love. On the Galilean shore, where Jesus had prepared breakfast for the disciples, He confronted Peter after they had eaten. "Jesus said to Simon Peter, 'Simon, son of Jonah, do you love Me more than these?' He said to Him, 'Yes, Lord; You know that I love You.' He said to him, 'Feed My lambs.' He said to him again a second time, 'Simon, son of Jonah, do you love Me?' He said to Him, 'Yes, Lord; You know that I love You.' He said to him, 'Tend My sheep.' He said to him the third time, 'Simon son of Jonah, do you love Me?' Peter was grieved because He said to him the third time, 'Do you love Me?' And he said to Him, 'Lord, You know all things; You know that I love You.' Jesus said to him, 'Feed My sheep,'" John 21:15-17. Peter's first love was restored.

The Savior's words to the members of the church at Ephesus are very soul-searching. "I have this against you . . . You have left your first love!"

Where is your first love? This is a searching question which we must ask ourselves and one another also today. We need the admonition of God's Word. The people in the congregation at Ephesus were not the first nor the last to lose their first love.

In his first Letter to the Corinthians, the apostle Paul writes about how the children of Israel often lost their first love. They all were rescued by passing through the Red Sea. They all were miraculously fed with food and water in the desert. God led them into the promised land of Canaan. Yet, how often they lost their first love and complained and grumbled against Moses and against God.

After the apostle Paul gives a lengthy report on how often the Corinthians lost their first love, he gives us a word of admonition, "Let him who thinks he stands take heed lest he fall," I Corinthians 10:12. We too can lose our first love. It happens when we put God and His Word on the back burner. Give God the first place in your life. The Savior expressed it this way in the Sermon on the Mount: "Seek first the kingdom of

God and His righteousness, and all these things shall be added to you," Matthew 6:33.

"He who has an ear, let him hear what the Spirit says to the churches." Do you have an ear to hear, that is, are you listening? It is the Spirit of God who speaks to us through His Word. Let us take His Word to heart.

There are three R's in our text – remember, repent, and return! First, remember God's love for you. Remember that God sent His Son, the Lord Jesus Christ, who always put God's will first and fulfilled the Law of God in our place. Remember that He took upon Himself all of our sins and suffered and died on the cross at Calvary to make a sacrifice for our forgiveness. Remember that He rose from the tomb and conquered sin, death and hell for us. He first loved us. Let us repent of the many times that we have failed to show our first love for Him. Let us repent of the times that our love for Him grew cold.

Let us keep our faith and trust in Him as God's Son and our Savior and He will warm our cold hearts! Let us turn and return to Him and then we have the promise of His blessing for time and for eternity. When we turn to Him and trust in Him, by the grace of God we overcome. Through our faith in Him we eat from the tree of life and we have His promise of dwelling with Him in Paradise eternally. AMEN!

For further thought and discussion:

◆ What conditions, positive or negative, were exemplified in the Church at Ephesus?

◆ Each of the Letters that Jesus wrote follows a similar outline. Can you identify it? What application does this formula have to your life today? (Page 30)

◆ While it is evident that God recognizes and values our good works, what lesson do we have from the Letter to the Church at Ephesus to show that our good works are not enough? (Pages 34-35)

◆ What – or who – is to be our first love? (Page 35)

◆ We see many examples in Scripture of those who lost their first love in times of pressure. In your heart, have you ever been further from Christ than you should have been? (Pages 36-37)

◆ What are the three R's that bring us back into fellowship with God? (Page 38)

"A CHURCH BOTH POOR AND RICH!"

Revelation 2:8-11

Our sermon today is the third in a series that deals with the Letters written to the seven churches in Asia Minor. It was written by the evangelist John while he was in exile on the island of Patmos located off the coast of present day Turkey.

In the previous sermon, we considered the Letter written to the church at Ephesus, a church that was highly commended by the Lord but then also a church that was severely taken to task because it was a church which had lost its first love.

Today, we turn our attention to the Letter written to the church in Smyrna, a present day thriving seaport known as Izmir in western Turkey with a population of about 375,000.

The theme that I have chosen for the Letter to the church at Smyrna might seem to be somewhat contradictory, but it is not. The theme is:

"A CHURCH BOTH POOR AND RICH!"

We read this Letter in the Book of Revelation, chapter two, verses eight through eleven: "And to the angel of the church in Smyrna write, 'These things says the First and the Last, who was dead, and came to life: I know your works, tribulation, and poverty (but you are rich); and I know the blasphemy of those who say they are Jews and are not, but are a synagogue of Satan. Do not fear any of those things which you are about to suffer. Indeed, the devil is about to throw some of you into prison, that you may be tested, and you will have tribulation ten days. Be faithful until death, and I will give you the crown of life. He who has an ear, let him hear what the Spirit says to the churches. He who overcomes shall not be hurt by the second death.'"

PART I: A CHURCH THAT WAS SUFFERING

Unlike the Letter written to the church at Ephesus, the Letter to the church at Smyrna does not contain any criticism of the members. It is a Letter containing only commendation and praise. We might say that the church at Smyrna was what we would call a model congregation.

However, because it was a congregation of very faithful people, they had to suffer all kinds of persecution as many others did in the early Christian church.

The Savior spoke to them through this Letter and

said, "I know your works, tribulation, and poverty."
While the congregation was located in a seaport where
business was thriving, the members of the
congregation were basically poor people. Being
Christian people, they certainly were not poor because
they refused to work. But because they were
Christians, they were persecuted and taken advantage
of by the clever, shrewd and wealthy people in the
business world. Because of their Christianity, they
were not accepted socially in the community. Their
religion was ridiculed. Their Savior was slandered.

Of course, such a report should not really
surprise us. Even today, being a Christian is not
popular with the people who are worldly-minded.
There are many atheistic and anti-Christian
movements throughout the world, including our own
country. Pick up any newspaper or magazine and read
the editorials and the letters to the editor and you soon
learn how uncomfortable people are with the teachings
of Christianity and you learn about the hatred they
have for it.

Here is a brief summary of the thinking expressed
by anti-Christian people. Prayer is called a
superstition. Gathering in God's house for worship, as
we are doing this morning, is regarded as being a
waste of time. Following Christian principles is looked
upon as being narrow-minded. Believing what the

Bible teaches is said to be evidence that one is uneducated.

Such remarks are made to intimidate Christians and to silence the voice of Christian witness. In the face of all this, what should we do? Should we just keep quiet and let loud-mouthed critics have the last word?

We must remember that the Savior expects us to be witnesses for Him. Remember that the Savior never promised His followers that life would be a bed of roses or that Christians would have a carefree career. As He spoke to the Christians at Smyrna, "You will have tribulation," so He has also warned His followers for every generation, "In the world you will have tribulation; but be of good cheer, I have overcome the world," John 16:33.

The Christians at Smyrna were assured that the Lord saw and knew what was going on. "I know the blasphemy of those who say they are Jews and are not, but are a synagogue of Satan." The Christians in Smyrna were persecuted by people "who say they are Jews and are not." They were Jews according to their race, but they were not Jews according to their faith. They did not believe the promises of God with reference to the promised Messiah. They did not believe in Jesus Christ as their Lord and Savior. They were in the service of Satan.

In a number of his Epistles, the apostle Paul

discusses this same subject. In the Epistle to the Romans he wrote, "He is not a Jew who is one outwardly . . . but he is a Jew who is one inwardly," Romans 2:28-29. Later in that same Letter he wrote, "They are not all Israel who are of Israel, nor are they all children because they are the seed of Abraham," Romans 9:6-7. In the Letter to the Galatians, the apostle Paul wrote, "Therefore know that only those who are of faith are sons of Abraham . . . Those who are of faith are blessed with believing Abraham," Galatians 3:7,9.

You and I, who believe that Jesus Christ is our Lord and Savior, really believe as Abraham believed and we are called the children of Abraham, even though we are not Jews according to the flesh.

What happened in Smyrna reminds us of the people who once said to Jesus, "'Abraham is our father.' Jesus said to them, 'If you were Abraham's children, you would do the works of Abraham. But now you seek to kill Me, a Man who has told you the truth which I heard from God. Abraham did not do this. You do the deeds of your father.' Then they said to Him, 'We were not born of fornication; we have one Father – God.' Jesus said to them, 'If God were your Father, you would love Me, for I proceeded forth and came from God; nor have I come of Myself, but He sent Me. Why do you not understand My speech? Because you are not able to listen to My Word. You are of your father the devil, and the desires of your father you want to do. He was a murderer from the beginning, and does not stand in the truth, because there is no truth in him. When he speaks a lie, he speaks from his own resources, for he is a liar and the father of it,'" John 8:39-44.

They were like people today who claim they are Christians, but they really are not. They may have their names written on a Christian church roster somewhere, but they really do not believe what the Christian Church teaches, namely, that we are saved by God's grace for Christ's sake through faith alone. And they do not live like Christians either. They often live like little devils! Such church members bring shame upon the name of Christ and His Church.

The people in the congregation at Smyrna were told that there were even more sufferings that they would face because of their Christian faith. "Indeed, the devil is about to throw some of you into prison, that you may be tested, and you will have tribulation ten days." We have the saying, "Forewarned is forearmed!" Some, indeed, ended up in prison because they confessed their Christian faith and, indeed, they needed a word of comfort.

PART II: A CHURCH THAT WAS COMFORTED

Indeed, their faith would be tested, but at the same time they were told that God would put limits on the testing. "You will have tribulation ten days." The Book of Revelation is written with a great deal of symbolic language and symbolic numbers. Ten days refers to a rather limited time and it really points to a period of short duration.

When our faith is tested and tried, we must remember and cling to God's promises in His Word. Recall His promise expressed in the First Epistle to the Corinthians. "No temptation has overtaken you except such as is common to man; but God is faithful, who will not allow you to be tempted beyond what you are able, but with the temptation will also make the way of escape, that you may be able to bear it," I Corinthians 10:13.

For the strengthening of your own faith, read chapter eleven of the Letter to the Hebrews. There you read that the faith of God's children was tried and tested down through the centuries. We read of the faith of Noah, Abraham, Sarah, Isaac, Jacob, Joseph, Moses, Rahab, Gideon, Samson, Samuel, David, Daniel and others. Their faith was tried and tested but they trusted the promises of a gracious God, "(Who) Himself has said, 'I will never leave you nor forsake you.' So we may boldly say: 'The Lord is my Helper; I will not fear. What can man do to me?'" Hebrews 13:5-6. The author of the Epistle to the Hebrews is quoting Psalm 118:6.

Continuing in the faith, the people of the congregation in Smyrna were told, "Do not fear any of those things which you are about to suffer." They really had nothing to fear because God was with them, and as Scripture assures us, "If God is for us, who (or what) can be against us? He who did not spare His own Son, but delivered Him up for us all, how shall He not with Him also freely give us all things? . . . It is Christ who died, and furthermore is also risen, who is even at the right hand of God, who also makes intercession for us. Who shall separate us from the love of Christ? Shall tribulation, or distress, or persecution, or famine, or nakedness, or peril, or sword? . . . In all these things we are more than conquerors through Him who loved us. (And then he concludes with those triumphant words:) I am persuaded that neither death nor life, nor angels nor principalities nor powers, nor things present nor things to come, nor height nor depth, nor any other created thing, shall be able to separate us from the love of God which is in Christ Jesus our Lord," Romans 8:31-32,34-35,37-39.

Why could the members of the congregation in Smyrna, and also we, speak with such conviction?

Because it is the almighty Son of God who is among us, as it is said in the introduction to the Letter: "These things says the First and the Last, who was dead, and came to life." He is the First and the Last. He is the eternal Son of God. He is the only Savior who is speaking. This is He who was dead. He suffered and died on the cross to redeem us and to save us from sin, death, and hell. But He came back to life. He rose from the dead and came forth triumphantly from the tomb. He is our risen Redeemer and ever-living Lord. The victorious Christ in whom we believe is speaking. And He urges us, "Be faithful until death," and He promises us, "I will give you the crown of life."

We are encouraged to be faithful to our Lord until our dying day, and we have His promise, "I will give you the crown of life." The crown of life is eternal life, God's gift to all who believe and trust in Christ as their Lord and Savior. What a beautiful contrast we have in these words.

We will be given a crown of glory. Here in this life we may be poor, but there we will be rich; here we may be in rags, but there we will wear a beautiful wreath; here we may suffer persecution, but there we will enjoy complete victory! By faith we make God's gift our very own. Just think; by faith in Christ we are rich. By faith we will enjoy the riches and blessings of heaven. By faith we conquer. We have nothing to fear.

The Letter draws to a close with the promise, "He who overcomes shall not be hurt by the second death." What is meant by the second death? This is the first time that this expression, "second death," appears in the Book of Revelation, and later it is explained that the second death is hell, everlasting separation from God. However, the members in the congregation at Smyrna and also we are told that we need not be filled with fear. "He who overcomes shall not be hurt by the second death." If you are faithful until death, that is, physical death, if you continue in the faith until the day you die, then you need not fear eternal death.

This Letter to the church at Smyrna, as all the Letters to the seven churches, closes with the words, "He who has an ear, let him hear what the Spirit says to the churches." This is an emphatic way of saying, "Please listen! Please, pay attention! Please take these words to heart!" Then you have the promise of God's blessing, the promise of eternal life. You may be poor physically, but what riches will be yours in heaven! AMEN!

For further thought and discussion:

◆ What conditions, positive or negative, were exemplified in the Church at Smyrna?

◆ At no time has it been easy to follow Jesus. What are some examples of the way the world seeks to minimize, ridicule, or intimidate Christians today? (Pages 42-44)

◆ What words does Jesus have for people who attend church and claim to be Christians, but don't truly believe or follow the Word of God? (Pages 45-46)

◆ When trouble or testing comes, what assurance do we have that we will have the strength to overcome? (Page 47)

◆ Revelation 2:10 states, "Be faithful until death, and I will give you the crown of life." What does this mean to you? (Page 49)

◆ What is meant by the phrase, "He who has an ear, let him hear what the Spirit says to the churches?" (Page 50)

"A CHURCH IN A DANGEROUS SETTING!"
Revelation 2:12-17

This morning, we direct our attention to the third of the seven Letters sent to the seven churches in Asia Minor. In the Letter to the church in Ephesus we learned about a church that was commended for some things and also rebuked because it was a church that had lost its first love. In Smyrna the church consisted of members who were both poor and rich, poor in physical things but rich in spirit.

This morning, as we journey in spirit to the city of Pergamos, we find,

"A CHURCH IN A DANGEROUS SETTING!"

We read about this church in the Book of Revelation, chapter two, verses twelve through seventeen: "And to the angel of the church in Pergamos write, 'These things says He who has the sharp two-edged sword: I know your works, and where you dwell, where Satan's throne is. And you hold fast to My name, and did not deny My faith even in the days in which Antipas was My faithful martyr, who was killed among you, where Satan dwells. But I have a few things against you, because you have there those who hold the doctrine of Balaam, who taught Balak to put a stumbling block before the children of Israel, to eat things sacrificed to idols, and to commit sexual immorality. Thus you also have those who hold the doctrine of the Nicolaitans, which thing I hate. Repent, or else I will come to you quickly and will fight against them with the sword of My mouth. He who has an ear, let him hear what the Spirit says to the churches. To him who overcomes I will give some of the hidden manna to eat. And I will give him a white stone, and on the stone a new name written which no one knows except him who receives it.'"

PART I: SOME REMAINED FAITHFUL

In the text before us we have the earliest record of a Christian Church located in Pergamos. We have no knowledge of any one specific person under whose leadership the congregation was organized. Next to Ephesus at that time, Pergamos appears to have been the most prominent city in Asia Minor. As best as we know, its last king did not have any descendants and he turned the city over to the Romans.

In many ways, Pergamos was what we today would call a tourist town, and it was visited by many ancient pilgrims. It also was a city that was very popular for its many heathen temples. It had temples dedicated to the worship of many and various heathen gods, including a temple or a number of temples dedicated to Roman rulers including Caesar Augustus.

To establish a Christian congregation in a place surrounded by a number of heathen temples was, indeed, a dangerous setting. Those dangerous surroundings were recognized by the Lord, who said, "I know your works, and where you dwell, where Satan's throne is." The Christian congregation was located in an area of the city called Satan's throne, a place where the devil was having a heyday.

It was dangerous to live where the heathen zealots sacrificed to idols and also where they engaged in all kinds of sexual immorality. It might well have been located in the part of town where they had what we today would call adult pornography shops and houses of prostitution, or what in years gone by was more commonly known as the "red light" district.

I am sure that you would agree, that's a dangerous setting for the location of any church! However, in that area, which was called Satan's throne and the place where Satan dwells, a Christian church was established where the Christian message of salvation by God's grace through faith in Jesus was proclaimed and preached.

Dangerous as the setting was, there still were

faithful church members in that congregation and community. In the letter addressed to the pastor and the congregation at Pergamos, the Lord Jesus said, "You hold fast to My name, and did not deny My faith even in the days in which Antipas was My faithful martyr, who was killed among you, where Satan dwells."

The danger of living in that community is emphasized by the report that Antipas was a faithful Christian martyr. He was killed because he confessed the Christian faith. We have no further information about this Antipas. This is the only place in the Bible where his name is mentioned. There is a legend that he was burned alive in a heated metal image of a bull. However, that is only a legend dating back to the tenth century. It is not something that is recorded in Holy Scripture.

Nevertheless, in spite of being persecuted in Pergamos by the followers of heathen religions, who were in the service of Satan, there were those who remained faithful to the Christian faith. Several expressions are used to stress their faithfulness - "You hold fast to My name," and, "(You) did not deny My faith."

Theirs was not a secret Christianity. Their faith was not something that they just kept to themselves. When it comes to confessing Christ as our Lord and

Savior, silence is not the way to go. Yet, far too often Christians are silent when they should be confessing their faith.

Often we are silent because we are either ashamed or afraid to confess that Jesus Christ is the Son of God and the only Savior for all sinners. We believe that Jesus is our Savior who has delivered us from sin, death and hell, and we also believe that He is the only Savior also for others. When we believe that there is no salvation "In any other, for there is no other name under heaven given among men by which we must be saved," Acts 4:12, then we must be ready to confess Him.

Remember also the words of the Lord Jesus Himself, "I am the Way, the Truth, and the Life. No one comes to the Father except through Me," John 14:6. Jesus always identified Himself as the only Savior for sinners.

Remember what the apostle Paul wrote about Christ in his Letter to the Philippians, "(Christ Jesus) humbled Himself and became obedient to the point of death, even the death of the cross . . . God also has highly exalted Him and given Him the name which is above every name, that at the name of Jesus every knee should bow, of those in heaven, and of those on earth, and of those under the earth, and that every tongue should confess that Jesus Christ is Lord, to the glory of

God the Father," Philippians 2:8-11. That is what we confess. Such was the Christian faith of many members of the congregation in Pergamos.

The faithfulness of some members of the congregation at Pergamos reminds us of how they also heeded what was written to some of the other churches in Asia Minor. For example, the ending of the Letter to the Church at Smyrna reads, "Be faithful until death, and I will give you the crown of life," Revelation 2:10, and the ending of the Letter to the Church at Philadelphia reads, "Hold fast what you have, that no one may take your crown," Revelation 3:11. Everything else can come and go, but hang on to your Christianity!

PART II: SOME FALL FOR SATAN'S LIES

However, as in every generation, there were in Pergamos those who fell for Satan's lies. In his Letter to the Romans, the apostle Paul wrote about those who fall from and reject the Christian faith, and he refers back to the time of the prophet Isaiah. He writes, "They have not all obeyed the Gospel. For Isaiah says, 'Lord, who has believed our report?'" Romans 10:16.

In Pergamos there were those who became victims of the heathen and ungodly surroundings. In the Letter we read, "I have a few things against you, because you have there those who hold the doctrine of

Balaam, who taught Balak to put a stumbling block before the children of Israel, to eat things sacrificed to idols, and to commit sexual immorality . . . You also have those who hold the doctrine of the Nicolaitans, which thing I hate."

The story of Balaam and Balak goes back to Old Testament times. Balaam persuaded Balak to set a spiritual deathtrap for the children of Israel. Balak convinced many of the children of Israel to participate in the idol worship and in the idol feasts and celebrations of their day. At those celebrations, after they had eaten and drunk too much, they engaged in sexual immorality with the heathen temple prostitutes, both men and women.

In addition to that, some people in the congregation at Pergamos also had embraced the false teachings of the Nicolaitans. We heard about them in the Letter to the church at Ephesus. Exactly what they taught and believed we do not know. However, their teachings and practices are put into the same category as that of Balaam, and the whole intent was to lead the children of God astray. It was an attempt to lead the children of God away from the truth and away from the worship of the true God and to lead them to worship the idols of this world where Satan rules and dwells. As I said earlier, indeed, the church in Pergamos was in a dangerous setting!

But really it is no different today. Wherever there is a Christian Church and a Christian community, the devil takes up a residency next door! The devil never takes a vacation. He never takes time out or time off! He is just as determined today to mislead and to lead astray the children of God.

That is why it is so important for us to heed the warnings of Scripture, "Be sober, be vigilant; because your adversary the devil walks about like a roaring lion, seeking whom he may devour. Resist him, steadfast in the faith," I Peter 5:8-9. "Put on the whole armor of God, that you may be able to stand against the wiles of the devil," Ephesians 6:11. "Resist the devil and he will flee from you," James 4:7.

We are urged to take these words to heart. Note who is speaking. "He who has the sharp two-edged sword." This is none other than the Son of God portrayed also as the Judge before whom we are all accountable. The two-edged sword is the Word of God including the Law of God that condemns and convicts us of sin. It also includes the Word of God that calls us to repentance and faith, as is done in the conclusion to this letter: "Repent, or else I will come to you quickly and will fight against them with the sword of My mouth."

This is a passionate plea: turn from sin, from false teachings and false teachers, from idolatry, from the ways of the world, and from sexual immorality, and from all the other temptations of Satan. Turn from sin to the Savior. Receive His assurance of forgiveness and receive from Him the power to resist and to conquer sin.

We should be equipped like soldiers of the cross. In his Letter to the Ephesians the apostle Paul pleads with faithful Christians with these words: "Put on the whole armor of God, that you may be able to stand against the wiles of the devil. For we do not wrestle against flesh and blood, but against principalities, against powers, against the rulers of the darkness of this age, against spiritual hosts of wickedness in the heavenly places. Therefore take up the whole armor of God, that you may be able to withstand in the evil day, and having done all, to stand. Stand therefore, having girded your waist with truth, having put on the breastplate of righteousness, and having shod your feet with the preparation of the Gospel of peace; above all, taking the shield of faith with which you will be able to quench all the fiery darts of the wicked one (that is, the devil). And take the helmet of salvation, and the sword of the Spirit, which is the Word of God," Ephesians 6:11-17.

The Word of God equips us and makes us conquerors with Christ. Of this victory, we are told in our text, "To him who overcomes I will give some of the hidden manna to eat. And I will give him a white stone, and on the stone a new name written which no one knows except him who receives it."

The hidden manna takes us back again to the Old Testament. Moses had stored up some of the manna in the Sanctuary and it became known as the hidden manna. It symbolized the coming Christ, Jesus, who called Himself the Bread from heaven.

Another blessing is promised to those who repent and accept Christ as Lord and Savior. "I will give him a white stone, and on the stone a new name written which no one knows except him who receives it." This is a gift signifying purity, the purity or the righteousness which is ours by faith in Christ. We also receive a new name. We are children of the heavenly Father by faith in Christ Jesus.

"He who has an ear, let him hear what the Spirit says to the churches." Please listen! Please take these words to heart! AMEN!

For further thought and discussion:

- What conditions, positive or negative, were exemplified in the Church at Pergamos?
- The Church at Pergamos was established in what is described as a very dangerous environment. What are some of the more dangerous environments for Christianity today? (Page 55)
- Have you ever felt that you let the opportunity to witness for Jesus slip by because of fear? If so, how did you feel afterward? (Page 57)
- As Christians, we are bombarded with the cares and ways of the world. What is our sure defense against sin and temptation? (Page 61)
- What was represented by the white stone at the end of the letter? Why is it important? (Page 62)

"A CHURCH THAT NEGLECTED DISCIPLINE!"
Revelation 2:18-29

This morning, we direct our attention to the fourth of the seven Letters written to the churches in Asia Minor. It is the Letter to the church in Thyatira. It seems a little strange that the congregation in that city, which was the smallest of the seven cities, should receive the longest of the seven Letters. It is also the most difficult of the seven Letters to understand, to interpret and to apply.

The theme that I have chosen for this Letter is:

"A CHURCH THAT NEGLECTED DISCIPLINE!"

This Letter is recorded in the Book of Revelation, chapter two, verses eighteen through twenty-nine: "And to the angel of the church in Thyatira write, 'These things says the Son of God, who has eyes like a flame of fire, and His feet like fine brass: I know your works, love, service, faith, and your patience; and as for your works, the last are more than the first. Nevertheless I have a few things against you, because you allow that woman Jezebel, who calls herself a prophetess, to teach and seduce My servants to commit sexual immorality and eat things sacrificed to idols. And I gave her time to repent of her sexual immorality, and she did not repent. Indeed I will cast her into a sickbed, and those who commit adultery with her into great tribulation, unless they repent of their deeds. I will kill her children with death, and all the churches shall know that I am He who searches the minds and hearts. And I will give to each one of you according to your works. Now to you I say, and to the rest in Thyatira, as many as do not have this doctrine, who have not known the depths of Satan, as they say, I will put on you no other burden. But hold fast what you have till I come. And he who overcomes, and keeps My works until the end, to him I will give power over the nations – 'He shall rule them with a rod of iron; they shall be dashed to pieces like the potter's vessels' – as I also have received from My Father; and I will give him the morning star. He who has an ear, let him hear what the Spirit says to the churches.'"

PART I: THE CHURCH WAS COMMENDED

There are two references in the Bible to the city of Thyatira, the one being here in the Book of Revelation and the other in the Book of Acts. The Bible mentions only two people by name who lived in Thyatira. Both of them were women. The one was Lydia of whom we read in the Book of Acts, "She was a seller of purple from the city of Thyatira, who worshiped God. The Lord opened her heart to heed the things spoken by Paul. And when she and her household were baptized, she begged us, saying, 'If you have judged me to be faithful to the Lord, come to my house and stay.' So she persuaded us," Acts 16:14-15.

The other woman was Jezebel mentioned in our text who was a lying, deceiving child of the devil, who did untold damage in the congregation at Thyatira. We will hear more about her activities in just a little while.

We do not know under whose leadership the congregation in Thyatira was organized. There are those who think that Lydia, who was a God-fearing businesswoman, and who was converted to Christianity in Philippi, went back home and served as an evangelist in her home town. That certainly is a logical conclusion.

The congregation in Thyatira was reminded in its Letter that it was accountable to God and that its activities came under the scrutinizing eyes of the Son of God. "These things says the Son of God, who has eyes like a flame of fire, and His feet like fine brass." We are reminded of the all-seeing eye of God. The brass feet are a symbol of one who rules and thus we also are reminded of His almighty power. The Lord keeps an eye on the activities of a Christian congregation. He always knows what is going on, be it good or bad.

In the Letter to Thyatira, Jesus said, "I know your works, love, service, faith, and your patience; and as for your works, the last are more than the first." The Letter goes into detail and the Son of God mentions five things in the congregation that were commendable.

Their love was something that came from the heart. Their loyalty and devotion to the Lord was genuine. They loved Him who first loved them. It was not only a matter of the mouth, but they showed their Christian love by what they did.

They were involved in Christian service. They served the Lord with gladness, as the psalmist urges us to do. They ministered to the needs of their fellow-Christians in the congregation. It was a congregation, as was the case so often in the early Church, where nobody went hungry. They shared and looked after the needy, the widows and the orphans, the aged, the sick and the suffering.

Unfortunately, today, in our society, many people think that service to others and to the needy in the community is the responsibility only of the government. It is not just the job of the government. Thank God when we have people in government today who urge people to walk across the street and to give a helping hand to those in need! We do not need legislation to show love and service. The Lord gave us that responsibility from the beginning of time as expressed in the words, "Thou shalt love thy neighbor as thyself."

What is the motivating force behind Christian service? Our Letter tells us that it is Christian faith. We have faith in our Lord and Savior Jesus Christ. We believe that Jesus loved us and sacrificed Himself for us, that He suffered and died to take away our sins, and that He rose again from the dead, to conquer sin, death and the devil for us. His love for us in which we trust is the compelling force that moves us to love others.

Such is the faith that moves us to go and tell others that He is their Savior too. This is a faith that cares about the whole person, about both soul and body. The Christian faith is not something inactive or dead; it is very much alive. It is alive in works, in love, in service, and in patience.

True Christians deal with one another in patience. Ah, yes, patience! Patience in dealing with the differences, the oddities, the idiosyncrasies, the stubbornness, the lovelessness, the carelessness, and the like, of one another.

After commending the congregation in Thyatira for all of these fine Christian virtues, the words are added, "The last are more than the first." That means they were growing in grace. Their performance of their Christian duties was improving. They were growing spiritually. Things were getting better in the congregation.

What about us? As a congregation, are we growing, not just in numbers, but spiritually? Are we spiritually stronger today than we were in the past? Are we growing in Christian works, love, service, faith and patience? Are we being better witnesses for our Lord and Savior? As a congregation, in many ways we can respond favorably. But at the same time, we must admit that there is also a lot of room for improvement. We set our sights higher and we strive for greater goals. We exercise our Christianity, and we go onward, forward, like soldiers of the cross!

PART II: THE CHURCH WAS REPROVED

All of this is very commendable, but then, too, there are problems at times. To the church at Thyatira, the Savior said, "Nevertheless I have a few things against you, because you allow that woman Jezebel, who calls herself a prophetess, to teach and seduce My servants to commit sexual immorality and eat things sacrificed to idols."

Here was the weakness in the congregation. They

lacked discipline. They tolerated a certain woman, Jezebel, in the congregation. She posed as a prophetess, as if God had sent her, as if she had a special revelation from God and was teaching the truth. But what she was teaching was called "the depths of Satan." She undermined the morality in the congregation. She convinced some people in the congregation to commit sexual immorality and to follow the worship of heathen idols.

How could people in a Christian congregation fall for that? At that time in history there was an antinomian movement. What does that mean? Antinomian means against the Law, a movement against the Law of God. There were people who thought that when they became Christians, the Ten Commandments, God's Law, did not apply to them anymore. They thought that they were free to do as they pleased.

There is an antinomian movement today in our own country. Get the Ten Commandments out of our schools, out of our government, out of society, yes, out of the churches! The ungodly claims of situation ethics, that the situation decides whether something is right or wrong, and that it is wrong to pass judgment upon anything people do, is all a part of the antinomian movement, a movement against the Law of God, against the Ten Commandments!

But the Lord warns, if you want to live as you please, if you want to ignore or challenge His Commandments, if you want to live in sexual immorality, if you want to make your body your god, if you want to live with eyes full of adultery and that cannot cease from sin, you are going to pay a price!

In the Thyatira Letter, the Lord said, "I will cast her into a sickbed, and those who commit adultery with her into great tribulation, unless they repent of their deeds. I will kill her children with death, and all the churches shall know that I am He who searches the minds and hearts. And I will give to each one of you according to your works." As God moved Moses to write, "Be sure your sin will find you out!" Numbers 32:23.

And it is no different today. All of the sexual diseases and the plague of AIDS are the consequence of all of the sexual immorality in our society. And what is the real cure? The cure is not in finding ways for people to sin safely! Don't be intimidated by educated ignoramuses, who try to tell you that what people do in their private lives is their business. The call of the hour should be, "Repent and change your ways. Change your lifestyle."

We are living in this sinful world, but we should not be of the world. We are urged to, "Hold fast what you have till I come." Continue in the faith. Hang on to your Christianity. Continue in the Christian faith until the Savior returns. Continue to put your faith and trust in the Lord Jesus Christ for forgiveness of all your sins and turn to God humbly and penitently for His grace and mercy.

When we repent and return to the Lord we are assured of a victory. It is not a victory of our own making. But we will enjoy the victory which the Son of God provides for us. In this Letter, the Son of God is shown as the victorious Lamb of God over sin and every evil. "'He shall rule them with a rod of iron; they shall be dashed to pieces like the potter's vessels' – as I also have received from My Father." This is a clear example of Scripture interpreting Scripture. This clearly is a reference to what was written by the psalmist a thousand years before Christ was born.

The psalmist wrote, "The Lord has said to Me, 'You are My Son, today I have begotten You. Ask of Me, and I will give You the nations for Your inheritance, and the ends of the earth for Your possession. You shall break them with a rod of iron; You shall dash them to pieces like a potter's vessel,'" Psalm 2:7-9.

The evil in this world, yes, the sinful world itself, will come to an end. The close of this Letter reminds us that Christ is coming again and that there will be a day of judgment. That is a fearful thought for the ungodly and for the people of this world. But for the children of God it has no terror. We have been redeemed by our Lord and Savior. There is a place in the heavenly mansions for us who believe and trust in the Lord Jesus as the Son of God and our Savior.

In our text, we have His promise, "I will give him the morning star." This expression, morning star, appears only twice in the Bible, here in our text and at the end of the Book of Revelation where Jesus calls Himself the bright and Morning Star. Now, we are told that He is going to give us the morning star. That is nothing other than the glories of heaven which are ours because of what He, the Morning Star, did for us.

In the Old Testament the prophecy was given that there would come a Star out of Jacob. Christ is that Star of Jacob, that descendant of Jacob, who came to bring light into a dark and dying world. When the Savior was born, the wise men from the east came to Jerusalem and said, "We have seen His star in the East and have come to worship Him," Matthew 2:2. Christ is the bright and Morning Star, the Light of the world, as He called Himself.

Through His Word, of which this Letter is a part, He comes to enlighten us. He calls us out of darkness into the marvelous, glorious light of the Gospel. He tells us how much He loves us, that He has forgiven us and made us members of His family. As children of

His, He asks that we discipline our lives according to His good and gracious will.

"He who has an ear, let him hear what the Spirit says to the churches." Let us listen to our Lord prayerfully! Let us hear and heed His Word carefully! Let us believe and follow Him faithfully! Please listen! Please pay attention! Please take these words to heart. AMEN!

For further thought and discussion:

- What conditions, positive or negative, were exemplified in the Church at Thyatira?
- The Church at Thyatira was known as a group of caring Christians. What expectation does the Lord have of us with respect to caring for the less-fortunate in our society? (Page 68)
- What should be the driving force behind good works and acts of service? (Page 69)
- What does the Bible teach about keeping the Law as it relates to Christian freedom? (Pages 71-72)
- What does this section of Revelation promise to believers who continue in the faith? (Pages 73-74)

"A LETTER TO A DYING CHURCH!"
Revelation 3:1-6

When speaking about some particular evil, illness or disaster, how often have you said, "I pray to God that that will never happen to me!"

Well, today, as we consider the fifth of the seven Letters written by the apostle John to the seven churches in Asia Minor, we pray that what happened to the church in Sardis will never happen to our beloved congregation. The unfortunate story of what happened in Sardis is recorded in,

"A LETTER TO A DYING CHURCH!"

The Letter is recorded in the Book of Revelation, chapter three, verses one through six: "And to the angel of the church in Sardis write, 'These things says He who has the seven Spirits of God and the seven stars: I know your works, that you have a name that you are alive, but you are dead. Be watchful, and strengthen the things which remain, that are ready to die, for I have not found your works perfect before God. Remember therefore how you have received and heard; hold fast and repent. Therefore if you will not

watch, I will come upon you as a thief, and you will
not know what hour I will come upon you. You have a
few names even in Sardis who have not defiled their
garments; and they shall walk with Me in white, for
they are worthy. He who overcomes shall be clothed in
white garments, and I will not blot out his name from
the Book of Life; but I will confess his name before My
Father and before His angels. He who has an ear, let
him hear what the Spirit says to the churches.'"

PART I: THE LETTER REPORTS THE SPIRITUAL CONDITION

From the outset, let me say that the Letter
addressed to the church in Sardis was not the kind of
letter which you anxiously wait to receive in the mail.
The congregation in Sardis, as a whole, was not
commended for anything. Only a few people in the
congregation were singled out for their faithfulness. In
general, most of the members of the congregation were
spiritually dead or in the process of dying!

Who would dare to pass such a judgment upon a
congregation? It was none other than the Lord Jesus,
the Author of all of the Letters, who was speaking.
"These things says He who has the seven Spirits of God
and the seven stars." The reference to the seven Spirits
of God and to the seven stars is simply an emphasis

upon the speaking of the Holy Spirit to the seven churches and to their seven pastors or leaders.

How the Lord viewed the people in the congregation was quite different from how the people of the surrounding community viewed them, as well as how the people of the congregation viewed themselves. The Savior said, "I know your works, that you have a name that you are alive." To the people of the community, the members of that congregation were popular. They were a church with a name. Maybe they had a big, beautiful church building. Maybe the people of the community were flocking to Sardis to hear some popular preacher. Maybe they had a smooth-running organization. It appeared to be an active congregation, a growing and going institution! "You have a name that you are alive!"

If they had had all of the newspapers, the radio, and the TV which we have in our day, the congregation at Sardis would have been in the headlines repeatedly! As far as the people of the community and the world were concerned, the congregation at Sardis really had things going for it.

But that was not how the Lord saw it. He said, "I know your works." The Lord could see through it all. He knew what was going on, and He knew that it was not good. "I have not found your works perfect before God." All of the motion and commotion that they were going through, all of the activity that was supposed to be a sign of being alive, all of the boasting and bragging of what they as a congregation did, did not impress God! "You have a name that you are alive," but then came the scathing indictment, "But you are dead!" Period! The Lord's message was blunt and to the point. The Lord was telling it the way it was! The real problem in the congregation did not come from the outside but from within!

We do not know anything about the congregation in Sardis other than what we have in the text before us. We do not know how the congregation started there. The city is not named as one visited by any of the apostles. This is the only place in Holy Scripture where reference is made to the city of Sardis.

From a few secular historical accounts, we learn a little about the city. We are told that it was a well-fortified city. It was built on a rock, and you could enter the city only from one side. On the other three sides, the rock formation made it impossible to enter. On the fourth side, the street leading into the city was so narrow that it could easily be defended by a few soldiers. It was referred to as the "City Unconquerable."

History also reports that it was a wealthy city. The Pactolus River flowed past the city, and in it people panned for gold. According to some historical records, Sardis was the first city in the world to mint gold coins for use in trade. It became the first gold market of the world.

Maybe those conditions had something to do with what happened in the congregation. Maybe they were like a lot of people today who are more concerned about the money market and about what happens on Wall Street and about the economy than they are about how spiritually rich or poor they are! As long as the economy is good, they think that they are really living. But to how many of them would the Lord say, "You are dead!"

In Sardis, most of the members of the congregation were spiritually dead. They thought that they were alive. They had the reputation of being alive. They had their names written on the roster of the church, but their names were not written in God's Book of Life. Most of the members had what we today call a paper membership!

How can it happen? It happened in the past and it happens today. There are congregations that suffer from a spiritual creeping paralysis. It comes gradually and subtly, but it does indeed come! Many have their names recorded somewhere on church books, but their Christianity is dead! Some seldom appear in God's house for worship, and when they do it is only a formality, going through the motions. How many once pledged allegiance to the Lord, but today they walk no more with Him. The message and the meaning of Christianity is gone. The Savior would write them a little note today, as He did to the congregation in Sardis, saying, "You think you are alive, but you are dead!"

PART II: THE LETTER CALLS FOR REPENTANCE

The Letter to the congregation in Sardis calls for three things – watchfulness, remembrance and repentance. "Be watchful, and strengthen the things which remain, that are ready to die." Many in the congregation were told, "You are dead!", while others were told, "(You) are ready to die!" Some were already dead and others were at the verge of dying spiritually. The call was to be spiritually watchful; it was the call to wake up and to strengthen the spark of hope that was left.

How is this done? By returning to the Lord who still loved them and who was ready and willing to assure them of His love and forgiveness. His forgiveness was assured in the words, "He who overcomes shall be clothed in white garments, and I will not blot out his name from the Book of Life; but I will confess his name before My Father and before His angels." To be clothed in white garments refers to being washed white in the blood of Christ which cleanses us from all sin. What comfort to be told that our names will be confessed before the heavenly Father and the angels. Recall the words of Jesus, when He said, "I say to you, there is joy in the presence of the angels of God over one sinner who repents," Luke 15:10.

We overcome and conquer sin and Satan, death and hell, through faith in Christ. We make His victory our victory. We trust in Him whose holy, precious blood has cleansed us from all sin. We believe in Him who has trampled Satan underfoot. We have our hope in Him who rose again from the grave, assuring us that, "Death is swallowed up in victory," I Corinthians 15:54. With our faith, hope, and trust in Him, we can say with Paul, "Thanks be to God, who gives us the victory through our Lord Jesus Christ," I Corinthians 15:57. Being spiritually watchful is a sign that one is not spiritually dead or dying. Being spiritually watchful keeps us spiritually alive through Christ. The Lord urges us, "Examine yourselves as to whether you are in the faith. Test yourselves. Do you not know yourselves, that Jesus Christ is in you?" II Corinthians 13:5.

Jesus Christ is in us and among us with His Word as He continues to plead with sinners. He does not close the door on us. He does not want to see people perish. That is why He adds the warning, "If you will not watch, I will come upon you as a thief, and you will not know what hour I will come upon you."

In these words the Savior is simply repeating what He said during His ministry, when He told His disciples, "As the lightning comes from the east and flashes to the west, so also will the coming of the Son of Man be," Matthew 24:27. He is speaking of that day of which the apostle Peter wrote, "The day of the Lord will come as a thief in the night, in which the heavens will pass away with a great noise, and the elements will melt with fervent heat; both the earth and the works that are in it will be burned up," II Peter 3:10.

God has appointed the day when Christ will return. You and I are called upon to be prepared against that day by faith in the precious promises of a gracious and forgiving God.

In addition to being spiritually watchful, we are called upon to repent, lest we die in our sins. The Letter urges, "Hold fast and repent!" Hold fast to what? Hold fast to God's Word and His promises. The Lord has no pleasure in seeing people spiritually dead or dying. He tells us in His Word, "'As I live,' says the Lord God, 'I have no pleasure in the death of the wicked, but that the wicked turn from his way and live. Turn, turn from your evil ways,'" Ezekiel 33:11. Turn is the same as repent. Turn to the Lord and live.

Don't keep on going the way that leads to death and damnation. "(The Lord is) not willing that any should perish but that all should come to repentance," II Peter 3:9. "(God) desires all men to be saved and to come to the knowledge of the truth," I Timothy 2:4.

Watchfulness and repentance are two things that follow remembrance. Remember God's revelation. Where does God reveal Himself? He reveals Himself in the whole creation, as the psalmist says, "The heavens declare the glory of God; and the firmament shows His handiwork," Psalm 19:1. Open your eyes and see God's hand in the creation of all things. This world did not just happen or come into being on its own. It came into being by God's design and through His almighty power.

God reveals Himself in history. Read the history in His Word and follow secular history and you will see what has happened to one nation after another that has rejected God. Study the history of Scripture, which tells us that, "Whatever things were written before were written for our learning, that we through the patience and comfort of the Scriptures might have hope," Romans 15:4.

God reveals Himself especially in His Word, Holy Scripture. That is why we place such emphasis upon searching the Scripture, as we will do again beginning next week in Sunday School and Bible Classes. Let's take advantage of these opportunities so that we will grow spiritually and remain a living church and avoid the danger of becoming a church that is dying or dead!

Let us strive to remain numbered with those of whom the Letter to Sardis speaks, "You have a few names even in Sardis who have not defiled their garments; and they shall walk with Me in white, for they are worthy." There were a few in the congregation in Sardis who did not have their names just on the church roster, but whose names were written in heaven in the Book of Life. They were not defiled. They were clean because they believed and trusted in the Lamb of God who has taken away the sin of the world.

The Letter to the church in Sardis closes as they all do with the words, "He who has an ear, let him hear what the Spirit says to the churches."

Please listen! Please pay attention! Please take these words to heart, so that, as a congregation, it may never be said of us, "You are dead or in the process of dying!" AMEN!

For further thought and discussion:

◆ What conditions, positive or negative, were exemplified in the Church at Sardis?

◆ The Church members at Sardis had fooled themselves and others into thinking they were successful, but Jesus saw through them. Have you ever witnessed a similar situation in churches today? (Page 79)

◆ What message does Jesus have for those who find themselves faced with those circumstances? (Page 82)

◆ What does God reveal about the power of repentance and forgiveness? (Pages 82-84)

◆ What lessons are you learning from this Letter that can be applied to your life today?

"THE CHURCH WITH THE OPEN DOOR!"
Revelation 3:7-13

The Lutheran Church often has been called the church of the open Bible. That is a designation of which we are not ashamed. It was the return to the open Bible that brought about the Reformation. Our Lutheran Confessions and teachings are placed side by side with the open Bible, so that all people can see that what we teach and what we believe is in harmony with what is taught in the Word of God as it is revealed in the Bible.

However, what we believe on the basis of the Bible is something that should not be kept for ourselves. We should not only be the church of the open Bible, but also the church with an open door to welcome others to see and hear about God's love for all people, as He reveals it in His holy Word.

In this seventh sermon in our series of the seven Letters to the churches of Asia Minor, we direct our attention to,

"THE CHURCH WITH THE OPEN DOOR!"

Our text is recorded in the Book of Revelation, chapter three, verses seven through thirteen: "And to the angel of the church in Philadelphia write, 'These things says He who is holy, He who is true, He who has the key of David, He who opens and no one shuts, and shuts and no one opens: I know your works. See, I have set before you an open door, and no one can shut it; for you have a little strength, have kept My Word, and have not denied My name. Indeed I will make those of the synagogue of Satan, who say they are Jews and are not, but lie – indeed I will make them come and worship before your feet, and to know that I have loved you. Because you have kept My command to persevere, I also will keep you from the hour of trial which shall come upon the whole world, to test those who dwell on the earth. Behold, I am coming quickly! Hold fast what you have, that no one may take your crown. He who overcomes, I will make him a pillar in the temple of My God, and he shall go out no more. I will write on him the name of My God and the name of the city of My God, the New Jerusalem, which comes down out of heaven from My God. And I will write on him My new name. He who has an ear, let him hear what the Spirit says to the churches.'"

PART I: A CHURCH WITH OPPORTUNITIES

Unlike the Church in Ephesus, the Church in Philadelphia had not lost its first love. Unlike the Church in Smyrna, it was not a Church both rich and poor. Unlike the Church in Pergamos, it was not a Church in a dangerous setting. Unlike the Church in Thyatira, it was not a Church that neglected discipline. Unlike the Church in Sardis, it was not a dying Church. Unlike the Church in Laodicea, which we will consider next week, the Church in Philadelphia was not a self-satisfied Church. In contrast to all the other six Churches in Asia Minor, the Church in Philadelphia was the Church with the open door.

This Church was located in the city of Philadelphia in Asia Minor. The name Philadelphia comes from two Greek words and it means the city of "brotherly love." According to historical accounts, the city was named in honor of two brothers. Their love, loyalty and devotion to each other was something to behold. In recognition of the love of the two brothers, the people named the city in their honor, Philadelphia.

The city was located in an area where earthquakes occurred quite frequently, and in the year 27 A.D., it was destroyed by an earthquake. Soon thereafter, it was rebuilt. It was a prosperous city. It was located along a direct route lying between the central plateau of Asia Minor and the seaport of Smyrna. Many people settled there and many business people, many prosperous people, passed through Philadelphia.

A Christian congregation was organized there, but we do not know by whom. Because of its location and its many contacts with people, it was a church with many opportunities for what we call evangelism and outreach. The members took advantage of the many opportunities to meet people and to witness to them of the Christian faith. Unlike the Church in Sardis, which was a dying Church, the Church in Philadelphia was very much alive.

At this point, we can't help but think of our own community, which is rapidly growing with people taking up residency and businesses being established. What an opportunity for our congregation to be a Church with an open door, a Church that meets and greets people and shares with them the Good News of God's love for all of us through Christ Jesus our Lord and Savior!

Let me also call attention to the fact that in the Letter to the Church in Philadelphia there is not a single word of rebuke to the people of the congregation.

Oh yes, the Letter contains words of rebuke, but those words are addressed to the people outside the congregation who refused the welcome of the open door.

The author of this Letter identifies Himself with the words, "These things says He who is holy, He who is true, He who has the key of David, He who opens and no one shuts, and shuts and no one opens." The holy, truthful, promised descendant of David, the promised Messiah and the Savior of the world, is speaking. The Author is He who said at His ascension, "All authority has been given to Me in heaven and on earth. Go therefore and make disciples of all the nations, baptizing them in the name of the Father and of the Son and of the Holy Spirit, teaching them to observe all things that I have commanded you; and lo, I am with you always, even to end of the age," Matthew 28:18-20.

The Letter reminds us of the King of kings and Lord of lords, the kingly One who by His suffering, death, and resurrection opened the door of the kingdom for people to enter. Through us, through our witness, He invites, He urges, He calls, He pleads with people to come. He promises, "That whoever believes in Him should not perish but have everlasting life," John 3:16. Furthermore, what He opens no one can close. The Savior says, "My sheep hear My voice, and I know them, and they follow Me. And I give them eternal life, and they shall never perish; neither shall anyone snatch them out of My hand," John 10:27-28.

At the same time, this is the same Jesus who says that He shuts and no one opens. To those who reject Him, despise Him, and refuse to believe in Him, and who turn their backs upon His open arms, He has this to say, "He who does not believe will be condemned," Mark 16:16.

Christ, the King, acknowledged what was going on in the congregation in Philadelphia. He said, "I know your works." He knew what they were doing. They were an active congregation, a congregation that was spiritually alert, and eager to work. The Lord placed before them many mission opportunities and they took advantage of them and became known in the city as the Church with the open door.

The Lord was pleased and approved of what they did. The hand of God was at work among them. He directed others to pass through the city because He knew there were people who would take advantage of the opportunities to evangelize and to witness to those with whom they came into contact.

Their willingness to witness for the Lord becomes even more significant when we consider another factor mentioned in our text: "You have a little strength, have kept My Word, and have not denied My name." They were not yet a large, affluent congregation; the congregation was small in number and of little means.

They were a little flock, but they were determined to do great things for God! They were loyal to the Lord's Word. They carefully guarded the truth of God's Word. They would not permit the heathen philosophies and the worldly ways to creep in to take over in the congregation.

Oh yes, there were problems and difficulties to face. From within, things were going well, but from without, there was opposition. There was another church in town with which they had to deal. It is referred to in the words, "Indeed I will make those of the synagogue of Satan, who say they are Jews and are not, but lie - indeed I will make them come and worship before your feet, and to know that I have loved you." There were those who claimed to be faithful Jews, but they were lying. They were Jews according to the flesh, but they were not faithful followers of Abraham because they rejected Christ and the promised Lord and Savior. They had their own house of worship, the synagogue, where they went through religious rituals, but it was of Satan, not of God.

The people in the Philadelphia congregation remained faithful in spite of the opposition of those who tried to silence their voices. The Lord told them, "You have kept My command to persevere." They did not give up. They knew that their Lord was greater than Satan and his followers, who were seeking to destroy them.

We also need to remember that the Lord is by our side when we witness for Him. Our witness will not be in vain. His Word is powerful, and it accomplishes its purpose. Through the prophet Isaiah He says, "As the rain comes down, and the snow from heaven, and do not return there, but water the earth, and make it bring forth and bud, that it may give seed to the sower and bread to the eater, so shall My Word be that goes forth from My mouth; it shall not return to Me void, but it shall accomplish what I please, and it shall prosper in the thing for which I sent it," Isaiah 55:10-11.

He wants us to remember that He places before us open doors and He gives us opportunities for service. He expects us to take advantage of those opportunities and to trust Him for a blessing.

PART II: A CHURCH THAT WAS BLESSED

The congregation in Philadelphia truly was a Church with many opportunities, and because they took advantage of those opportunities, they were also a congregation that was blessed.

Just as the Lord blessed them, so He also seeks to bless us. Just as they continued in the faith, so He also expects us to continue in the faith. He says, "Behold, I am coming quickly! Hold fast what you have, that no one may take your crown." The Lord speaks of His second coming at the end of the world. He reminds us that the time of the world is rapidly running out. Time does not have the same significance for God that it has for us. Our days are numbered. He asks us as He asked the Philadelphians to continue in the faith, to hang on to our Christianity, and to be prepared spiritually at all times by faith in Christ for His sudden return.

By faith in Him we have the promise of eternal life, which is the crown to which He refers. Earlier in the Book of Revelation, John had written, "Be faithful until death, and I will give you the crown of life," Revelation 2:10. Faithfulness has the promise of His blessing, both for time and for eternity. That no one may take your crown is the first of a number of promises made in our text. The Savior assures us of our salvation.

He does not say that our faith will not be tested. In fact, quite the contrary; He says, "I also will keep you from the hour of trial which shall come upon the whole world, to test those who dwell on the earth." When the trials and the tests come, as a gracious God, He will see us succeed. He asks us to be faithful, but at the same time, He promises, "God is faithful, who will not allow you to be tempted beyond what you are able, but with the temptation will also make the way of escape, that you may be able to bear it," I Corinthians 10:13. Again, He promises, "The Lord is faithful, who will establish you and guard you from the evil one," II Thessalonians 3:3.

Another promise is given in our text. "He who overcomes, I will make him a pillar in the temple of My God and he shall go out no more." Remember, earlier I said that Philadelphia was in an earthquake zone. That made the pillars and the walls of the city and the buildings quite unstable. But here we are told that with the help of God, the Christians in Philadelphia would remain steadfast pillars. They would not fall.

As Christians, the Lord wants you and me to be pillars. He wants us to stand secure and tall, letting our Christian light shine in a shaking and unstable, dark and dying world! As Christians, we should be a credit to Christ and His Church.

Another promise is expressed with the words, "I will write on him the name of My God and the name of the city of My God, the New Jerusalem, which comes down out of heaven from My God. And I will write on him My new name." We are Christians; that's our new name. We are followers of Christ. We are the children of God by faith in Christ Jesus. Right now, we are His. He made us what we are. He created us and He has redeemed us. He has sanctified and called us into His family. He has given us our new name. He has written His name on us and He has written our names in His Book of Life. We belong to Him! What a blessing!

The apostle Paul talks about this when he writes, "You are no longer strangers and foreigners, but fellow citizens with the saints and members of the household of God, having been built on the foundation of the apostles and prophets, Jesus Christ Himself being the chief cornerstone, in whom the whole building, being fitted together, grows into a holy temple in the Lord, in whom you also are being built together for a dwelling place of God in the spirit," Ephesians 2:19-22.

This Letter closes with the same words as each of the others: "He who has an ear, let him hear what the Spirit says to the churches." Please pay attention! Please listen! Please take these words to heart. Let there be brotherly love! Let that love show itself as we take advantage of the open doors to witness for Him to others. Remember, as we take advantage of these open doors, we have the promise of His blessing. AMEN!

For further thought and discussion:

◆ What conditions, positive or negative, were exemplified in the Church at Philadelphia?
◆ The Church at Philadelphia was very much alive! What are some characteristics of Christians and Christian churches that are thriving? (Page 92)
◆ What mission and evangelism opportunities has God placed in your church's path recently? In what activities are you currently involved? Can you do more? (Page 96)
◆ As we work to share the Gospel and build the Kingdom, what promises does Jesus offer us? (Pages 97-99)

"A CHURCH THAT WAS LUKEWARM!"
Revelation 3:14-22

This morning, in thousands of churches throughout the length and breadth of our land, some reference will be made to the terrorist attack of this past Tuesday, 9/11. However, I would hope and pray that Christian clergymen would not spend the time just repeating the horror stories of TV and other media reporters. This is a time to hear the voice of Him who says, "Be still, and know that I am God," Psalm 46:10.

Christian pastors have a different message to proclaim, a message that is far more important and much more needed in an hour such as this, a message much more comforting and encouraging than anything the public press has to offer.

We, this morning, will continue with our series of sermons based upon the Letters written to the seven Churches in Asia Minor, which, incidentally, has something to say to us for such a time as this. We direct our attention to the last of the seven Letters. It is the Letter to,

"A CHURCH THAT WAS LUKEWARM!"

We read of this Church in the Book of Revelation, chapter three, verses fourteen through twenty-two: "And to the angel of the church of the Laodiceans write, 'These things says the Amen, the Faithful and True Witness, the Beginning of the creation of God: I know your works, that you are neither cold nor hot. I could wish you were cold or hot. So then, because you are lukewarm, and neither cold nor hot, I will vomit you out of My mouth. Because you say, 'I am rich, have become wealthy, and have need of nothing' – and do not know that you are wretched, miserable, poor, blind, and naked – I counsel you to buy from Me gold refined in the fire, that you may be rich; and white garments, that you may be clothed, that the shame of your nakedness may not be revealed; and anoint your eyes with eye salve, that you may see. As many as I love, I rebuke and chasten. Therefore be zealous and repent. Behold, I stand at the door and knock. If anyone hears My voice and opens the door, I will come in to him and dine with him, and he with Me. To him who overcomes I will grant to sit with Me on My throne, as I also overcame and sat down with My Father on His throne. He who has an ear, let him hear what the Spirit says to the churches.'"

PART I: THE CHURCH'S SPIRITUAL CONDITION

Laodicea was a prosperous city located in Asia Minor. A Christian congregation had been established there. The Apostle Paul was concerned about this congregation and he expressed the hope that his Epistle or Letter to the Colossians would also be circulated and read among the members of the Laodicean congregation.

About forty years later, the Laodicean congregation received its own Letter through the apostle John, who was directed to write to all seven churches in Asia Minor.

As we have seen during the past six weeks, each congregation received a Letter that dealt with its own specific spiritual needs. The Church in Ephesus had lost its first love, but the love in the Church in Laodicea was lukewarm. The Church in Smyrna was neither rich nor poor, but the Church in Laodicea was neither hot nor cold. The Church in Pergamos was in a dangerous setting, but the danger in the Church in Laodicea came from within. The Church in Thyatira neglected discipline, and the Church in Laodicea was satisfied with everything as it was. The Church in Sardis was a dying Church, but the Church in Laodicea was in a spiritual coma. The Church in Philadelphia was the Church with the open door, while the Church in

Laodicea was satisfied with things as they were and had slammed the door shut!

Our text tells us that the members of this congregation were neither hot nor cold spiritually. They were lukewarm. What did that mean? Had they been hot, they would have been Christians with hearts filled with faith and burning with the love of Christ. Had they been cold, they would have been hardened unbelievers without a spark of faith and love for Christ their Lord.

To be spiritually lukewarm means that they were neither hot nor cold. It's like people who really don't want to be in the Church, but who really don't want to be considered out of it either. Spiritually, such people are what we would call middle-of-the-roaders, or we might call it being a "political" Christian, one who walks the middle of the road and who tries to smile and please those on both sides.

But spiritually there is no such thing as a middle ground. The Lord Jesus said, "He who is not with Me is against Me, and he who does not gather with Me scatters abroad," Matthew 12:30.

The Laodiceans were lukewarm. Referring to them, the Savior expressed a wish which on first thought might seem somewhat unusual to us. "I could wish you were cold or hot." It is best to be a believer, but it would be better to be a known unbeliever than to play the part of a hypocrite. Outwardly, the Laodiceans tried to show warmth, but inwardly they were cold. While outwardly many of them went through a religious ritual, inwardly they had lost their faith.

They belonged to those of whom the Apostle Paul wrote, people "Having a form of godliness but denying its power," II Timothy 3:5. They said of themselves, "I am rich, have become wealthy, and have need of nothing." In their own minds they had reached the top and they were proud of it. They thought they had everything and knew everything. As far as they were concerned, there was no room and no need for any kind of improvement.

But God saw things differently. He said, "(You) do not know that you are wretched, miserable, poor, blind, and naked." Spiritually, that is not a very good picture! Of course, it would not be a good picture physically either – to be wretched, miserable, poor, blind, and naked! They thought that they were in pretty good shape, but they were wretched and miserable. They thought that they were wealthy, but they were miserably poor. They thought that they could see, but they were blind. They thought that they were well-clothed, but they were naked.

While they may well have prepared for their bodies, they failed to provide for their souls. While they had an abundance of earthly possessions, their souls were starving! Spiritually, they were naked; they had nothing to cover their sins. Yet, even in that condition, they felt satisfied; they were neither hot nor cold; they were lukewarm.

The generation of lukewarm church people did not die out with the Laodiceans. There are still many of them around today. This is another one of those letters that moves you and me to pray that what happened to the Laodiceans may never happen to us. We pray that we might never become a lukewarm church, a group of people who just plod along, neither hot nor cold, but just lukewarm spiritually! May we never become church people who say, "Who cares? We are rich and wealthy and need nothing!" God would respond differently: "You are wretched, miserable, poor, blind, and naked!" Lord, may it never happen to us, that we become spiritually lukewarm!

The lukewarm church member is like a halfhearted painter who puts his brush away after a rough sketch. He will never produce a glorious picture. He is like a composer who closes the cover to the piano keyboard after the first lesson. He will never produce a musical masterpiece. Likewise, the lukewarm church member will never set the church on fire spiritually. Each of these examples is a rather disgusting situation.

That is how the Lord viewed the Church in Laodicea. God was moved to speak a sentence of divine disgust. They were neither hot nor cold. They were lukewarm, and the Lord said, "It is nauseating for Me!" "I will vomit you out of My mouth!" Figuratively speaking, it actually made God sick to observe the condition in the Laodicean congregation.

PART II: WHERE WAS THE CHURCH'S HOPE?

In view of the Savior's words that may seem so harsh and severe, was there any hope for the Laodiceans? Oh yes! Christ still cared about them. He said, "As many as I love, I rebuke and chasten. Therefore be zealous and repent." It was love for their souls that moved the Lord Jesus to instruct the apostle John to send this Letter to them. It was love for their souls that moved the Savior to plead with them to repent. When the word "repent" appears alone in the Bible, it includes two things – true sorrow for sin, and faith in the Lord Jesus Christ as God's Son and our Savior.

Today, He would also invite us to repent and believe on the Lord Jesus Christ as our Savior. He would invite us as He invited the Laodiceans to become spiritually rich and clothed and healed. "I counsel you to buy from Me gold refined in the fire, that you may be rich; and white garments, that you may be clothed, that the shame of your nakedness may not be revealed; and anoint your eyes with eye salve, that you may see." Buy gold from Him! What's the price? It's free! Believe on the Lord Jesus Christ and the riches of heaven are yours. Receive from Him white garments. Be clothed and cover your sinful nakedness. Be robed in the white garments of Christ's righteousness. His righteousness covers all our sin. Anoint your eyes with eye salve so that you can see spiritually. Come out of spiritual blindness; be enlightened by the glorious Gospel of Jesus Christ, who suffered, died, and rose again to deliver us from sin, death, and hell.

When, in spirit, you stand at the foot of the cross and behold Him suffering and dying, and when at the open empty tomb you behold your risen Redeemer, is there any doubt as to how much He loves you and how much He really cares? The very fact that He keeps on coming to us in and through His Holy Word and the Sacrament is evidence of His marvelous mercy, His love, grace and forgiveness.

This is also impressed upon us both at the beginning and the ending of the Letter. It is not a letter from just anybody. It's a Letter from the Lord Jesus Christ. He identifies Himself with the words, "These things says the Amen, the Faithful and True Witness, the Beginning of the creation of God." This is the almighty Son of God, true God with the Father and the Holy Spirit, the Creator of heaven and earth, the Faithful and True Witness, the God who cannot lie, the Amen, who says, "So shall it be!"

At the end of the Letter you have that beautiful portrait of the Son of God portrayed in the words, "Behold, I stand at the door and knock. If anyone hears My voice and opens the door, I will come in to him and dine with him, and he with Me." This is a picture, I am sure, most of you have seen. If you have forgotten what it looks like, step into the sacristy after the service and look at the stained glass window. It's the painting of Jesus knocking at the door.

Today, the Savior stands at the door of your heart and mine. He is knocking and calling us to repentance and faith. He invites, "Believe on the Lord Jesus Christ," and He promises, "You will be saved," Acts 16:31.

Sometimes He calls and knocks in different ways and even in ways that we do not understand. Through the terrorist attack on Tuesday in our country, He is knocking at the door of hearts throughout America. It's a wake-up call for our whole country. We have often boasted that we are a Christian country. But many things that are said and done are far from being Christian. Thousands of our forefathers came to this country for freedom of religion, but today, many more thousands are clamoring for freedom from religion as they try to get every reference to God out of our country, out of our schools, out of our government, and, would you believe, even out of the churches!

The Savior says, "Behold, I stand at the door and knock!" America, wake up before it's too late!

The Letter closes with the promise of a blessing. "To him who overcomes I will grant to sit with Me on My throne, as I also overcame and sat down with My Father on His throne." Christ overcame! He suffered and died to redeem us. He rose triumphantly from the grave and He conquered sin, death and the devil. He ascended on high and He rules from heaven's throne.

We also are asked to overcome so that we might be with Him before His throne in heaven. How do we overcome? In his First Letter or Epistle, John answers this. "Whatever is born of God overcomes the world. And this is the victory that has overcome the world – our faith. Who is he who overcomes the world, but he who believes that Jesus is the Son of God?" I John 5:4-5.

By faith we make His victory our victory! And we have His personal promise that He will keep us in the faith. "My sheep hear My voice, and I know them, and they follow Me. And I give them eternal life, and they shall never perish; neither shall anyone snatch them out of My hand," John 10:27-28.

"He who has an ear, let him hear what the Spirit says to the churches." Please listen! Please take these words to heart! AMEN!

For further thought and discussion:

♦ What conditions, positive or negative, were exemplified in the Church at Laodicea?

♦ Many churches water down their message in an attempt to be all things to all people. What does Jesus say about those who try to walk the middle of the road in their spiritual life? (Pages 104-107)

♦ Have you ever visited a lukewarm church? Have you ever been lukewarm yourself?

♦ God only corrects those he loves. How does God's love shine through in each of these Letters? What message does He have for us? (Pages 107-111)

♦ Of the seven churches we've studied, which most resembles the church you attend now?

♦ What practical advice have you received from the Book of Revelation? What advice can you share with others?

PUBLISHER'S AFTERWORD

Every now and again, the opportunity presents itself to be part of something truly amazing. At those times, our work collides with passion and mission and purpose, and ceases, as it were, to resemble work at all. A labor of love, maybe . . . but certainly not work.

Love Letters from Jesus is one of those opportunities – a real-life dream come true for an independent publisher whose founding was based on a vision to influence beyond the material and to impact beyond the temporal.

The book you are holding – the book you have just finished reading – has its simple roots in the faithful fulfillment of a pastor's calling. What began as an interesting and instructive sermon topic soon became a powerful eight-part sermon series. Prayerfully researched and written by Pastor Leonard Buelow, it was then delivered to his congregation over the course of a two-month study more than a decade ago.

Interestingly, the events of September 11, 2001, events that would forever alter the American consciousness, discussion, and view of what was considered normal – what was considered safe – took place between sermon number seven and sermon number eight. That became apparent to you as you read the opening remarks to the final sermon on page 101.

Nevertheless, the hard truths and beautiful promises of the Word of God endure. The vision given to John by Jesus – yes, the *Love Letters from Jesus* – are as relevant and meaningful to His children today as when they were delivered to the churches of Asia Minor at the close of the first century.

The simple answer to the fears and challenges we face today are contained within the timeless words of Christ. The expectation that the Lord has for each of His children – for each of us – hasn't changed one iota in the thousands of years since they were spoken and recorded.

No doubt, in each of our lives there is much to be commended. We strive to do well – to do good – and this is admirable. It comes with the territory. At the same time, in our thoughts, words, and deeds, in our homes, workplaces, and churches, there is much left to be desired – for which to be admonished and rebuked. And plenty for which we must daily repent and seek forgiveness.

This sermon series makes one fact undeniably clear. The Book of Revelation is not a confusing jumble of dreams or visions that are impossible to discern or understand. On the contrary, it contains the beautiful letters of love from our all-powerful and caring Savior.

"He who has an ear, let him hear . . ."

Steve Buelow
New Media Jet, LLC.
Publisher

ABOUT THE AUTHOR

*"Be faithful until death, and I will give you
the crown of life." Revelation 2:10*

The Rev. Leonard P. Buelow is a passionate
and dedicated pastor and theologian whose
entire life and ministry can be summarized by the
phrase, "Called to Serve the Lord!"

While still in his youth, he was identified by his
own pastor as possessing many attributes of an
honorable and humble servant of the Word, including:

♦ the perseverance and will required to stand
firm in the commands and admonitions of the Lord

♦ the compassion and strength to lead God's
children back to the source of all truth in times of both
joy and heartache, and

♦ the ability to deliver powerful and life-giving
messages based solely on God's Law and the saving
grace that comes to all believers through the Gospel of
Jesus Christ.

To date, he has written and delivered nearly ten
million words of hope and inspiration to the hundreds
and thousands of Christian brothers and sisters whom
he has served.

Faithful to his calling, Pastor Buelow is presently
serving Amazing Grace Lutheran Church, a new
mission congregation in Green Bay, WI, where he
resides with Carola, his wife of nearly 60 years.